# About Your TRAINER

Gerard Braud is an award winning former journalist and author of *Don't Talk to the Media Until...29 Secrets You Need to Know Before You Open Your Mouth to a Reporter*. From 1979 to 1994, his career included job experiences in television, radio and newspaper.

He has been a news anchor, reporter, photographer and editor. First on the scene at many disasters of national consequence, Gerard was often called upon by CBS, NBC and CNN to provide coverage to the networks and their affiliates.

Because the "sound bite" or "quote" is the core of every news story, one of his most difficult tasks as a reporter each day was watching people struggle to articulate their points, especially during on-camera interviews. In 1986 he began developing the media training courses he teaches today. Each helps individuals avoid embarrassing and costly mistakes that are repeated daily by executives and spokespeople everywhere.

Since 1994, Gerard has worked on five continents as an expert in media training and crisis communications.

2621 Lakeshore Drive • Mandeville, LA 70448
985-624-9976 (New Orleans)
gerard@braudcommunications.com
www.braudcommunications.com
© 2019 Braud Communications

# The Philosophy of
# MEDIA TRAINING

# IF...

# "If you could attach a dollar to every word that comes out of your mouth, would you make money, or would you lose money?"

Gerard Braud
Braud Communications

An interview is an opportunity. It is as important as any business deal or decision that affects the bottom line of the company, organization, or agency.

_____
_____
_____
_____
_____

*Read Lesson 2 of Don't Talk to the Media Until...*
*to learn more about the Philosophy of Media Training.*

2621 Lakeshore Drive • Mandeville, LA 70448
985-624-9976 (New Orleans)
gerard@braudcommunications.com
www.braudcommunications.com
© 2019 Braud Communications

# Don't Talk to the Media... Talk to the Media's Audience

- Who is watching television?
- Who is listening to the radio?
- Who is reading the newspaper?
- Who is getting their news from the web?
- Who is getting their news from social media?
- Who is getting their news from mobile devices?
- What is their education level?
- What is their level of cynicism?
- What is their attention span?

The average person watching television news has a _____ grade education. (U.S. Based)

The average person reading a newspaper has a _____ grade reading level. (U.S. Based)

*Read Lesson 1 of Don't Talk to the Media Until... to learn more about the media's audience.*

# Who Are the Media?

The media are the messengers to the masses.

They can only report what they know.

It is up to you to give them all of the facts as you know them to be true.

If you don't give them the facts they will get the facts from someone else.

That "someone else" may not see the facts the way you do.

The more you know about the media, the less intimidated you will be.

2621 Lakeshore Drive • Mandeville, LA 70448
985-624-9976 (New Orleans)
gerard@braudcommunications.com
www.braudcommunications.com
© 2019 Braud Communications

# What Do the Media Want?

They want a hot story.

They want to make a name for themselves.

They want to be recognized among their peers for having the lead story.

They want a story that will help them advance their careers.

Their producers, editors and news directors want them to have stories that will draw viewers to their newscast, listeners to the radio or readers to their publications or websites.

They crave death, destruction and powerful images - "If it bleeds, it leads!"

*Read Lesson 11 of Don't Talk to the Media Until...*
*to learn more about the people who don't see it as you do.*

# What Will the Media Say?

Reporters start with what they believe the facts to be.

These facts often represent a misconception.

These misconceptions are often mistaken as bias in the media.

This perceived bias occurs because editors and newsroom managers often send news crews out to do a report based on partial facts or information from a biased source.

Often, reporters arrive for a story only to call back to their news organizations to report that the story is nothing like they expected.

Reporters are told to keep talking to people until they get the "facts."

Your job is to present the facts in a way that is easy for the reporter to understand.

*Read Lesson 5 of Don't Talk to the Media Until...*
*to learn more about ignorance and bias by the media.*

2621 Lakeshore Drive • Mandeville, LA 70448
985-624-9976 (New Orleans)
gerard@braudcommunications.com
www.braudcommunications.com
© 2019 Braud Communications

# Practice: Morning Talk Shows

Interview Scenario:

- Local morning television talk show.
- The interviewer has been up since 3 a.m. and is sleep deprived.
- The interviewer is relatively young without worldly knowledge.
- The interviewer has not had time to read any background information about you or your company.
- The interviewer doesn't even know your name.
- The interviewer has prepared no questions.
- The interview will last just 3 minutes.
- Your job is to answer the interviewer's questions as best as you can.

# Body Language

**As we watch and review your video, please observe your body language. Here are some things the experts tell us to look for.**

- **DON'T rub your eyes or rub the tip of your nose.**
  This says you are being less than honest.

- **DON'T slouch in the chair.**
  This says you are too cavalier and you don't care.

- **DON'T sit with your hands folded in your lap.**
  This says you are vulnerable.

- **DON'T stand or sit with your arms folded.**
  This says you are being defensive.

- **DON'T sit in a chair with wheels or a chair that swivels.**
  You will rock or sway, which indicates you are nervous.

- **DON'T sway if you are standing during the interview.**
  Spread your legs a little farther apart than usual to give yourself a solid base.

- **Be careful how you cross your legs.**
  If you do cross your legs, DON'T let your leg swing.
  Don't expose the sole of your shoe to the camera.

- **DO sit with your arms open and relaxed on the arms of a chair.**
  This says you are relaxed, open and willing to be honest.

- **Do talk with your hands.**
  Upward facing hands say you are honest and open.
  Talking with your hands will help to relax you.

*Read Lesson 27 of Don't Talk to the Media Until...*
*to learn more about body language and how to sit.*

2621 Lakeshore Drive • Mandeville, LA 70448
985-624-9976 (New Orleans)
gerard@braudcommunications.com
www.braudcommunications.com
© 2019 Braud Communications

# Review Video & Evaluation

What general observations do you have about your interview and your performance?

___

What questions do you have about your interview and your performance?

___

Who controlled the interview?

___

While you were talking and answering questions, what were you wondering in your mind?

___

While you were answering questions, what do you think the interviewer was thinking?

___

How might you gain greater control over the interview?

___

*Read Lesson 6 of Don't Talk to the Media Until...*
*to learn more about controlling each question.*

# Taking Control

- Control begins when you always know the first 2 sentences you will say at the beginning of your interview, regardless of the question.

- Consider your first 2 sentences to be a preamble to your conversation.

- Your first 2 sentences must provide context to the conversation.

- Your first 2 sentences must be intelligent, conversational and quotable.

- Your first sentence must establish the noble purpose for the existence of your company, including how you serve the greater good of humanity.

- Your second sentence must tell us 3 ways you serve humanity (products/services) and must give us "poster child" examples of who it is that you serve, how and for what purpose.

- Your second sentence outlines for the audience the 3 key areas you are prepared to discuss.

- Both sentences must be focused on the value and benefits you provide to external audiences and not internal audiences.

> Example: At ABC Natural Resources, our goal is to build a stronger world. We do that by exploring for oil and gas used to fuel your car and heat your home; we do that by exploring for vital minerals, such as gold and copper, used in many of the electronics you use every day; and we do that by researching alternative energy, to power the world of the future for our children and grandchildren.

*Read Lesson 9 of Don't Talk to the Media Until...*
*to learn more about key messages.*

2621 Lakeshore Drive • Mandeville, LA 70448
985-624-9976 (New Orleans)
gerard@braudcommunications.com
www.braudcommunications.com
© 2019 Braud Communications

# Key Message

- Next, you will write and learn a series of phrases that will be called your "Key Messages."
- Key Messages are intelligent, conversational and quotable sentences that let you communicate your thoughts in a clear, logical pattern.
- Key Messages instantly give you words to say while your brain thinks of the rest of the answer.
- Key Messages serve as a mental outline or road map for your interview.
- Key Messages should not be memorized, but internalized.
- Key Messages are easiest to internalize when thoughts are clustered in 3's.
- Key Messages serve as a defense mechanism when you are asked negative questions.
    - They provide a place for you to retreat to verbally.
    - They re-establish context to your answers.
    - They give you words to say while your brain thinks of the rest of your answer.

# Key Message Tree

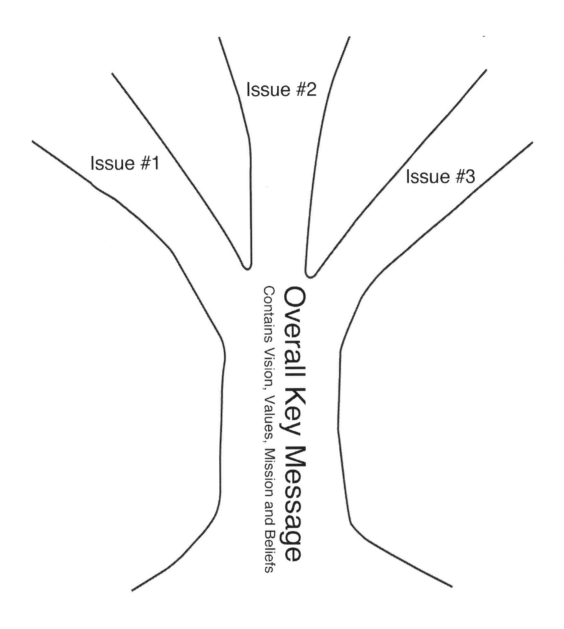

*Read Lesson 29 of Don't Talk to the Media Until...
to learn more about the myth of 3 key messages.*

2621 Lakeshore Drive • Mandeville, LA 70448
985-624-9976 (New Orleans)
gerard@braudcommunications.com
www.braudcommunications.com
© 2019 Braud Communications

# Sample Key Message Tree

Tree Trunk (Preamble)

Example: At ABC Natural Resources, our goal is to build a stronger world. We do that by exploring for oil and gas used to fuel your car and heat your home; we do that by exploring for vital minerals, such as gold and copper, used in many of the electronics you use every day; and we do that by researching alternative energy, to power the world of the future for our children and grandchildren.

Branch (Issue) #1: Oil & Gas

In the area of oil and gas, our goal is to find untapped reserves to support our current economy; to remove those minerals from deep within the earth in the safest way possible so that the environment is protected; and to refine the minerals into the natural gas used to heat homes and businesses, or the gasoline you purchase when you drive up to the pump.

- Limb 1: Exploring for reserves
- Limb 2: Production
- Limb 3: Usable products

Branch (Issue) #2: Copper & Gold

Branch (Issue) #3: Alternative Energy

# Your Key Messages

Tree Trunk (Preamble)

At _____ our goal is to _____ .

We do that by _____ ;

We do that by _____ ;

And we do that by _____ .

Branch (Issue) #1:

_____

_____

_____

Branch (Issue) #2:

_____

_____

_____

Branch (Issue) #3:

_____

_____

_____

2621 Lakeshore Drive • Mandeville, LA 70448
985-624-9976 (New Orleans)
gerard@braudcommunications.com
www.braudcommunications.com
© 2019 Braud Communications

# Grow Your Key Message Tree

- **Grow your key message tree with additional writing, 2 sentences at a time.**

    Every Branch can grow 3 Limbs.

    Every Limb can grow 3 Twigs.

    Every Twig can grow 3 Leaves.

    Allow your tree to grow sweet fruit - your stories.

- **Each limb, twig and leaf grows from the previous sentence.**

    Use simple A-B-C 1-2-3 explanations.

    Make every additional sentence quotable and able to stand on its own.

    Don't rush to add excessive facts and details.

    Don't use technical terminology.

    Don't use corporate jargon.

    Don't use acronyms.

    Use analogies to explain complicated issue.

    Cluster examples into groups of 3 and never give a long list of examples.

*Read Lesson 8 of Don't Talk to the Media Until...*
*to learn more about why too many facts are bad.*

# Controlling Questions & Answers

- Your key messages give you control over your answers.

- To control questions, you must take your thinking to a higher level.

- To control the next question, you must create a level of suspense at the end of your answer. Writers describe this as a "Cliff Hanger" sentence.

    Example Answer: Branch (Issue) #1: Oil & Gas

    In the area of oil and gas, our goal is to find untapped reserves to support our current economy; to remove those minerals from deep within the earth in the safest way possible so that the environment is protected; and to refine the minerals into the natural gas used to heat homes and businesses, or the gasoline you purchase when you drive up to the pump.

    Example "Cliff Hanger."

    I think you'd be surprised to learn some of the ways we're now able to find untapped reserves...

- What will the next question be?

    Example Interviewer Question:

    What are some of the ways that you're are finding untapped reserves?

*Read Lesson 6 of Don't Talk to the Media Until...*
*to learn more about what the next question will be.*

2621 Lakeshore Drive • Mandeville, LA 70448
985-624-9976 (New Orleans)
gerard@braudcommunications.com
www.braudcommunications.com
© 2019 Braud Communications

# How Reporters Write a News Story

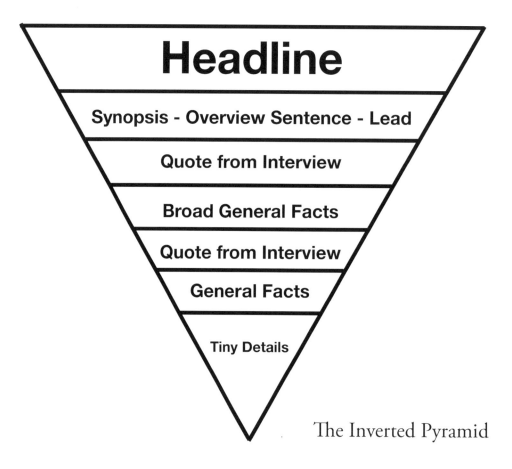

The Inverted Pyramid

*Read Lesson 3 of Don't Talk to the Media Until...*
*to learn more about how reporters write.*

# Anatomy of a TV News Story

| Lead | Sound bite | Transition | Sound bite | Stand up | Conclusion |
|---|---|---|---|---|---|
| :15 | :15 | :15 | :15 | :15 | :15 |

# Anatomy of a Print News Story

| Lead | Quote | Transition | Quote | Facts | Conclusion |
|---|---|---|---|---|---|
| One Sentence | One Sentence | Two Sentences | One Sentence | Two Paragraphs | |

*Read Lesson 3 of Don't Talk to the Media Until...*
*to learn more about how reporters write.*

# Basic Rules for Conducting an Interview

- Be honest.
- Never say "no comment."
- Keep to your message.
- Keep your answers short.
- Avoid answers that include "but."
- Do not speculate.
- Do not answer hypothetical questions.
- Do not speak for someone or something else.

- Be proactive.
- Be positive.
- Be prepared with facts and figures.
- Keep promises to get facts you don't have.
- Be responsive and understanding to deadlines.

- In television, do an interview before the interview while the camera crew is setting up.
- Never speak off the record.
- Assume that the camera is always rolling and the microphone is always recording.

*Read Lesson 14 of Don't Talk to the Media Until...*
*to learn more about how reporters speculate.*

# Distractions

- **Where to look during the interview?**

- **DON'T be distracted by the camera lens.**
    Always talk to and look at the reporter during your interview.
    If your eyes shift back and forth from the reporter to the camera, it indicates you are uncomfortable and may be telling a lie.

- **DON'T let your clothing be a distraction to the audience.**
    Avoid loud colors and complicated patterns.
    Women should avoid flowered patterns.
    Men should avoid loud neck ties.

- **DO wear studio makeup in a studio if it is offered to you to avoid distracting shine.**

- **When meeting your interviewer, DON'T be star-struck.**
    The ego of each reporter is different.
    Some hold their jobs because they enjoy being recognized and they enjoy celebrity status.
    Some reporters recognize they are professionals doing a job.

- **You should act professional and treat the reporter as a professional.**

- **AVOID comments such as, "You look taller on TV" or "You look much nicer in person."**
    Remember, your first impression of him/her is also his/her first impression of you.
    You are here for a purpose, not an autograph session.
    Stick to your messages.

*Read Lesson 26 of Don't Talk to the Media Until...*
*to learn more about how to dress for an interview.*

# Looks Are Important

- **Dress for the location.**

    In a television studio:
    Business attire is best.

    Jacket should be unbuttoned.

    In a casual setting:
    Khakis or similar casual clothing is best.

    Never wear a hat, helmet or cap during an interview.

- **Hair and makeup:**

    You should have a conservative haircut.

    For women, makeup should avoid bright reds, in favor of softer neutral colors.

    Consider having a professional makeover, if necessary.

    Men also need simple powder to avoid oily and shiny skin.

*Read Lesson 26 of Don't Talk to the Media Until...*
*to learn more about how to dress for an interview.*

# Practice Exercise Two

Interview Scenario:

- Local morning television talk show with easy questions.

- The interviewer is somewhat knowledgeable about what you do.

- The interview will last just 3 minutes.

- Your job is to answer the first question using your Tree Trunk Key Message.

- After delivering the Tree Trunk Key Message, add a "cliff hanger," designed to make the interviewer ask you a question that positions you to deliver your next key message, which would be Branch #1. Deliver the "cliff hanger" then stop talking.

- After delivering Branch #1, add another "cliff hanger" to make the interviewer ask you a questions that positions you to deliver Branch #2. Deliver the "cliff hanger," then stop talking.

- After delivering Branch #2, add another "cliff hanger" to make the interviewer ask you a question that positions you to deliver Branch #3. Deliver the "cliff hanger," then stop talking.

- After delivering Branch #3, work toward a conclusion.

- You may hold your paper with your key messages for this exercise.

- The goal is not to test your memorization skills, but to allow your brain and mouth to "test drive" your messages verbally, while attempting to achieve comfort with pre-determined answers.

# Review Video & Evaluation

Which interview was better for you? The first interview or the second interview?
_____

What comfort or discomfort did you have using your key messages and why?
_____

How successful were you in inserting "cliff hangers" to control the next question?
_____

What general observations do you have about your interview and your performance?
_____

What questions do you have about your interview and your performance?
_____

What will you do more of or differently in your next interview to improve?
_____

# Negative Interviews

- You MUST begin EVERY interview with your Tree Trunk and Branch Key Messages. This establishes your "Noble High Ground" and a safe place to retreat when negative questions are asked.

- Negative questions must never be answered directly, but must be initially answered with your previous "tree trunk" or "branch" key messages, so as to provide context to the answer you are about to give.

  (Remember the diagram about going back to your safe harbor.)

- Your answer must then continue on to answer the essence of the question without spin.

- Congruency is critical - If your key messages do not align with your actions, then your key messages will fail you and the interview will go poorly.

- Never volunteer negative information, then expect to erase it with positive information.

## Gerard's 3 Bucket Rule

Things We Must Say | Things We Will Only Talk About if Asked | Things We Cannot Discuss

# Preparing for the Negative Interview

- Schedule Media Training before the interview with emphasis on role-playing the questions in this specific interview

- You may need to write a new preamble that is specific to the interview.

- Develop a deep list of anticipated questions.

- Make sure your Tree Trunk and Branch Key Messages work for this interview.

- Do additional writing to add limbs, twigs and leaves to your Key Message Tree.

- Cultivate, practice and perfect the stories you will tell.

- Determine what analogies might help explain complicated issues.

- Revisit your 3 Bucket diagram.
  Develop a list of items that you "must say."
  Develop a list of the things you will only talk about if asked.
  List the things you cannot discuss and determine how you will answer if asked about them.

*Read Lesson 18 of Don't Talk to the Media Until...*
*to learn more about negative interviews.*

# How to Answer a Negative Question

The secret to answering a question is to answer it the way you wished it had been asked. Follow these rules:

- **Listen to how the question is phrased.**

- **You are not obligated to answer the question directly.**

- **Ask, "is that the way I wish the question had been asked?"**

- **Does the question contain a negative connotation?**

- **Mentally place the negative question in a positive context.**

- **Mentally ask yourself the question the way you wish it had been asked.**

- **Answer the question the way you wish it had been asked.**

# Wrong Answer vs. Right Answer

**QUESTION**

Dr. Jones, some say your research is a breakthrough for science. But isn't it true that your critics have poked a lot of holes in your theory?

**WRONG ANSWER**

Well, yes, I have some critics who say my theory is incorrect. But I don't believe it is. I stand by my research.

**RIGHT ANSWER**

The vast majority of the scientific community supports my theory. They do believe it is a breakthrough for science.

*Participants may use this quote in articles and instruction provided it is attributed to Gerard Braud.*

# "Someone is going to edit what you say. It might as well be you."

**Gerard Braud**
**Braud Communications**

_Participants may use this quote in articles and instruction
provided it is attributed to Gerard Braud._

2621 Lakeshore Drive • Mandeville, LA 70448
985-624-9976 (New Orleans)
gerard@braudcommunications.com
www.braudcommunications.com
© 2019 Braud Communications

# During the Interview...

- Make corrections if the reporter misstates a fact or implies a falsehood.
- If you do not know the answer, then say so.
- Avoid making "absolute" statements.
- Do not get angry.
- Bridge back to your key messages, when possible.

**BLOCK – BRIDGE – HOOK**

- Block negatives.
- Bridge to key message and safe harbor.
- Hook with new information.

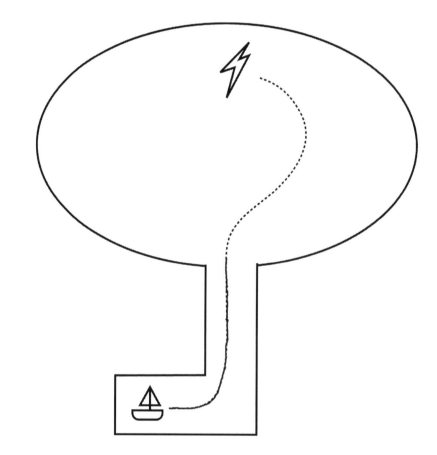

# Practice Exercise Three

Interview Scenario:

• This will be an interview that will be edited into a news report for either a newspaper, web publication or television newscast.

• The interviewer is a knowledgeable investigative reporter who is well prepared.

• The interview will last 3 - 5 minutes.

• Your job is to answer the first question using your Tree Trunk Key Message.

• After delivering the Tree Trunk Key Message or preamble, continue on to the appropriate branch and/or limb that will lead to your eventual answer.

• When you complete each answer, do your best to add a "cliff hanger," designed to make the interviewer ask you a question that positions you to deliver your next key message.

• Avoid answers in Bucket #2, where possible.

• Remember to Block negative questions by Bridging back to Key Messages and Hooking with new information.

# Review Video & Evaluation

What general observations do you have about your interview and your performance?
___

What comfort or discomfort did you have using your key messages and why?
___

How successful were you in inserting "cliff hangers" to control the next question?
___

Did you go into Bucket #2 and open the door to more negative questions?
___

What questions do you have about your interview and your performance?
___

What will you do more of or differently in your next interview to improve?
___

"If you could attach a dollar to every word that comes out of your mouth, would you make money, or would you lose money?"

Gerard Braud
Braud Communications

*Participants may use this quote in articles and instruction provided it is attributed to Gerard Braud.*

2621 Lakeshore Drive • Mandeville, LA 70448
985-624-9976 (New Orleans)
gerard@braudcommunications.com
www.braudcommunications.com
© 2019 Braud Communications

# What Next?

The skills used to talk to the media must be treated the same way a great athlete approaches their sport, i.e., the more you practice, the better you get.

- **Rx**
  Use your Key Messages every chance you get.
  Use them at least three times a day for the next three weeks.

- **Refresher Course**
  At a minimum, you should take a refresher course at least once a year.

- **Practice Before Every Interview**
  Role play with your public relations team or a colleague.

- **Develop more Key Messages**
  Develop an "Issues Library" filled with pre-written key messages.

- **Read *Don't Talk to the Media Until...***

- **Listen to one lesson of the audio CD each morning as you commute to work.**

- **Schedule a follow up call with Gerard to discuss your progress or any issues.**

Made in the USA
Monee, IL
29 January 2024

Made in the USA
Monee, IL
29 January 2024